5

But the two men had already walked away.
Georgie pushed a trolley over to her mum
and dad.

"What took you so long, Georgie?" asked Mum.

"Nothing."

"Come on," said Dad.
"We've got to check in. Then we
have to get on the plane."

Georgie Brown
- Hero

Stan Cullimore

When Georgie Brown got to the airport she was very excited. She was going on a trip to Jersey with her mum and dad.

"Georgie, can you go and get me a trolley?" said Dad.

Georgie went over to a line of trolleys. She pulled one away from the line and turned round.

"Hey, kid – watch where you are going!"

Georgie looked up. A short fat man was standing in front of her. Georgie had pushed the trolley into the man's bag.

"Sorry, I didn't see you," said Georgie.

The man turned to his friend.

"Stupid kid."

His friend, who was a tall thin man, nodded.

Georgie picked up the fat man's bag. Something fell out. Georgie bent down and picked it up. It was a gas mask. Georgie had never seen a real gas mask before. The fat man grabbed the gas mask.

"Give me that!"

He took the bag from Georgie and put the gas mask back inside it.

"Get lost, kid," said the tall man angrily.

"I'm really sorry," said Georgie.

Chapter Two

When they got onto the plane Georgie saw the short fat man. He was sitting in the row in front, next to the tall thin man. Georgie groaned. The plane started to race down the runway.

As soon as the plane was in the air Georgie stood up.

"I'm going to the toilet," she said.

She went to the back of the plane and into the toilet.

Chapter Three

A few minutes later Georgie opened the door and came out of the toilet. She walked back to her seat. She frowned. There was a funny smell in the air. Georgie looked around. All the people on the plane were asleep.

"That's funny. They were all wide awake a minute ago."

Georgie got back to her seat and sat down.
Her mum and dad were asleep in their seats.

"Now that is really odd," said Georgie to herself,
"Dad never goes to sleep on planes."

Just then, Georgie saw the short fat man in the
seat in front of her. The man was wearing the gas
mask that Georgie had seen in the airport. The
tall thin man was also wearing a gas mask. The
two men were wide awake. Georgie watched
them as they both took off their gas masks.

11

The two men stood up.

"Has the sleeping gas gone now?" asked the fat man.

The thin man nodded.

"Are all the people asleep?" asked the fat man.

The thin man looked around. Georgie closed her eyes as if she was asleep.

"Yes," said the thin man.

"Let's get the diamonds and go. Don't forget the parachutes," said the fat man.

Chapter Four

"Come on, cut the chain," said the fat man.

The thin man held up the case.

"Here it is."

The two men walked away from Georgie.
They went to the front of the plane,
towards the cockpit.

Georgie did not know what to do. She stood up and looked around to see if any of the other people on the plane were awake. But everyone was fast asleep. Georgie heard footsteps. The two men were coming back. She sat down and closed her eyes.

The thin man walked up to Georgie's seat and stopped.

"Goodbye, stupid kid. In a while you won't be so stupid anymore – you will be dead!"

"Come on, hurry up. We have to jump out of the plane," said the fat man.

Georgie heard the two men walk to the back of the plane.

A few seconds later she heard a loud noise and felt a rush of air on her face. Georgie jumped up and looked down towards the back of the plane. The two men had opened a door and were standing in the doorway.

As Georgie watched, the fat man jumped out of the door. The thin man waited for a few seconds and then he jumped after the fat man.

Georgie got out of her seat and went towards
the open door. Air was still rushing past her
face and making everything feel cold. Georgie
went over to the open door and got hold of it.
She pulled on the door as hard as she could.
Slowly the door began to move. It was hard
work but at last Georgie got the door shut.
Georgie looked around the plane.

"Now what do I do?" she said.

Chapter Five

As soon as she had said the words, Georgie knew what to do. She had to find out who was flying the plane! Georgie ran up towards the front of the plane, to the cockpit.

"Oh, no," she gasped.

The two pilots in the cockpit were fast asleep.

As Georgie stood looking at the two sleeping pilots the radio came to life.

"Come in, flight four two."

Georgie looked around. The pilots were wearing headphones. Georgie bent down. She took the headphones off one of the pilots and put them on her own head.

"Repeat, come in!"

The radio came over the headphones.

"Hello," said Georgie.

"Hello, flight four two. What is going on? You are flying the wrong way!"

Georgie gulped.

"I don't know what is going on. Two men put all the people to sleep with sleeping gas. Now they have jumped out of the plane and I am the only one who is awake."

"Who are you?" asked the radio.

"My name is Georgie Brown."

"Hello, Georgie. My name is John. Now listen to me, Georgie. If we do not do something fast, the plane is going to crash."

Georgie gulped.

"I need you to fly the plane," said John.

Georgie gulped again.

"Do you think you can do that, Georgie?"

"I'll try," replied Georgie.

"Good. The first thing you must do is sit down in a pilot's seat."

Georgie nodded. "OK."

She went over to one of the pilots and dragged him out of the seat. She sat down.

"Now what do I do?"

"Can you see a big green button?" asked John.

"Yes!"

"That is the main control button. You must press it and then take hold of the joystick with both hands," said John.

Georgie did as she was told. She felt the plane move.

"Well done, Georgie. You are now flying the plane," said John.

Chapter Six

The next few minutes were the longest minutes of Georgie's life. John told her what to do as she got used to flying the plane.

"You are doing really well," said John.

"It's easy to fly a plane, isn't it?" said Georgie.

"Well, the hard bit is landing."

Georgie gulped. She had forgotten about that.

"I'll never be able to land this plane," she said.

She started to feel scared, very scared.

"It won't be easy. But I can help you."

"But I don't know what to do," cried Georgie.

"Keep calm," replied John. "You are doing great. Now, can you see the airport in front of you?"

Georgie looked. A long way off she could see something that looked like a big wide road.

"There are lots of red lights by the side of the runway," said John.

As Georgie looked at the big wide road on the ground, lots of red lights came to life.

"Yes, I can see it," she cried.

Chapter Seven

"You must fly the plane down towards the runway," said John.

Then he gave Georgie a list of things to do. Georgie did them all.

"Good. Now the plane is ready to land," said John. "When I tell you to, you must press the big green button two times. The main controls will take over. They will land the plane."

"OK."

The plane got closer and closer to the runway. At last the radio came to life.

"Now, Georgie, press the button," said John.

Georgie pressed the button and closed her eyes.

A few seconds later the plane was on the ground, racing along the runway.

"Now press the three black buttons on your left," said John.

Georgie opened her eyes and pressed the three black buttons. There was a loud noise and she felt the plane start to slow down. After a few seconds, which seemed like hours, the plane came to a stop.

Georgie stood up and looked out of the window. She saw a truck racing up to the plane. There were some steps on top of the truck. The truck stopped so that the steps went up to the door of the plane. A man got out.

A few seconds later the door of the plane opened and the man came inside.

"Who are you?" asked Georgie.

"I'm John," replied the man. "And I know who you are. You are Georgie Brown – hero!"